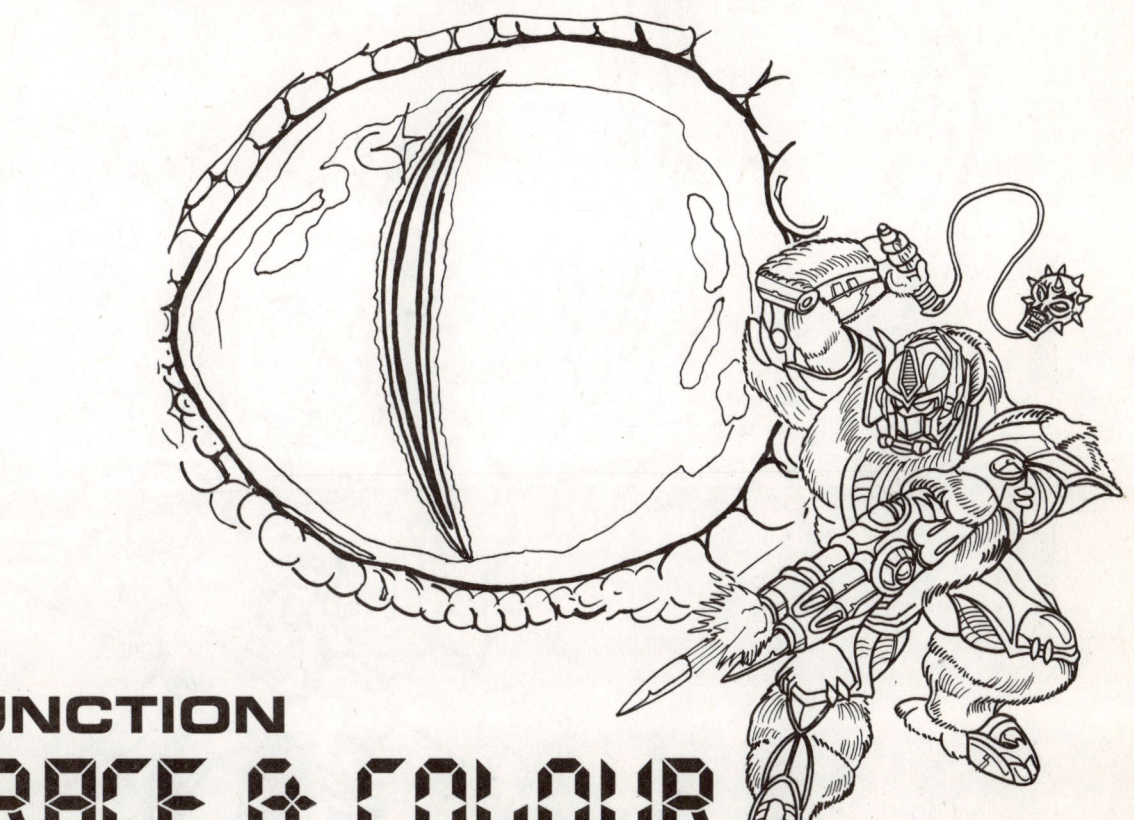

FUNCTION
TRACE & COLOUR

Pancake Press

ISBN 0 3303 6571 1

Published in Australia 1997 by Pancake Press,
an imprint of Pan Macmillan Australia Pty Ltd.
St. Martins Tower, 31 Market Street
Sydney NSW 2000
(ACN 001 184 014)

© 1997 Hasbro International Incorporated

Printed by Griffin Press

All rights reserved. No part of this book may be reproduced
without written permission from the copyright holder.

PREDACONS

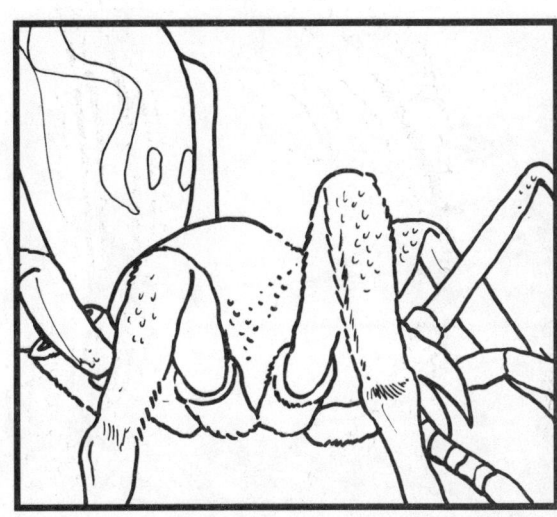

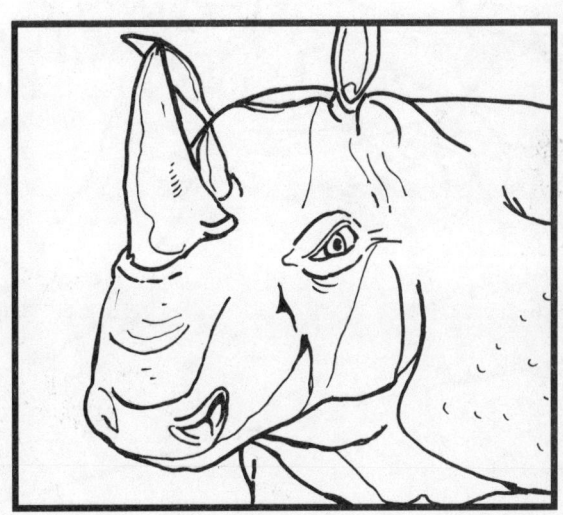

MAXIMALS

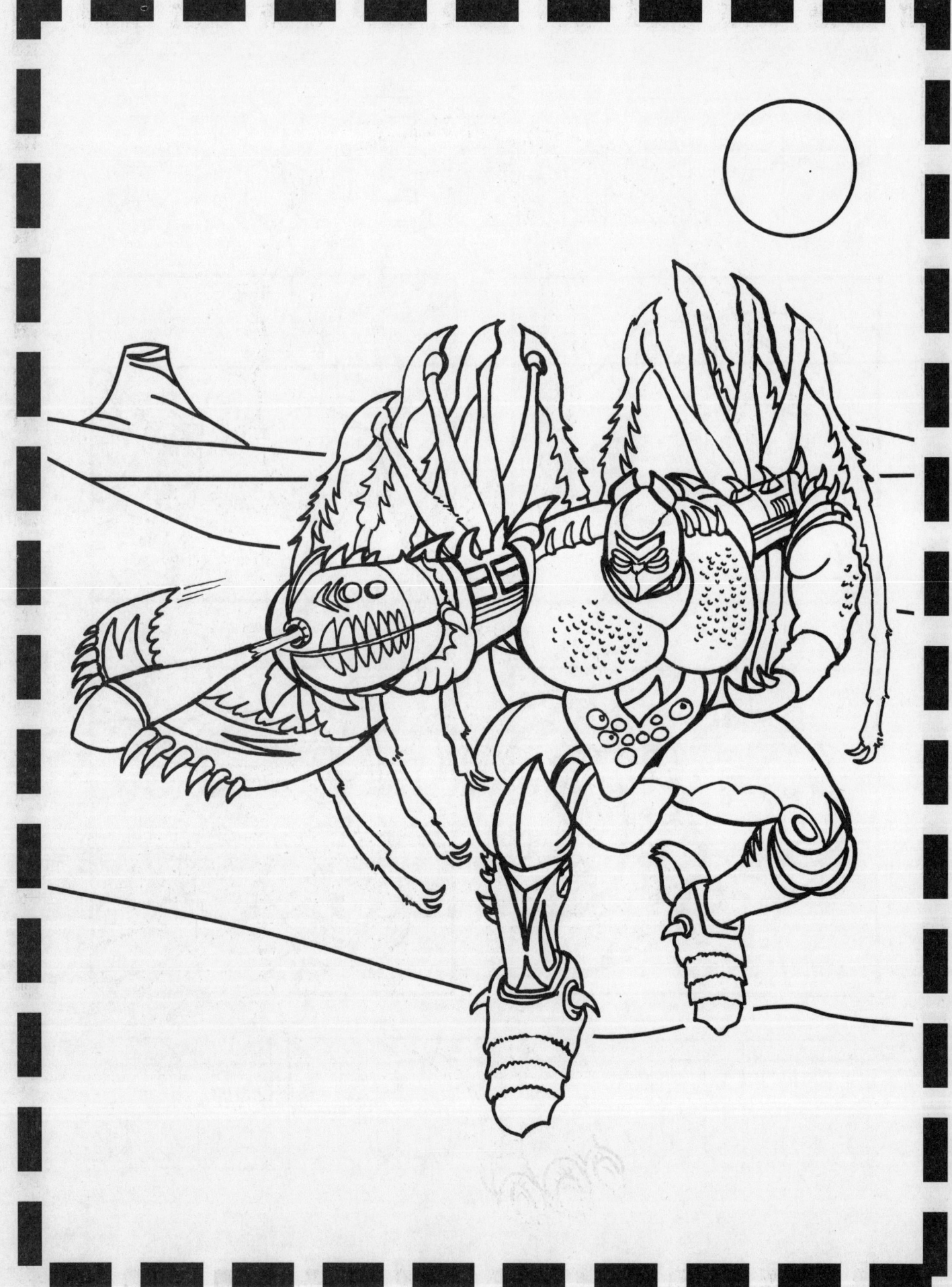

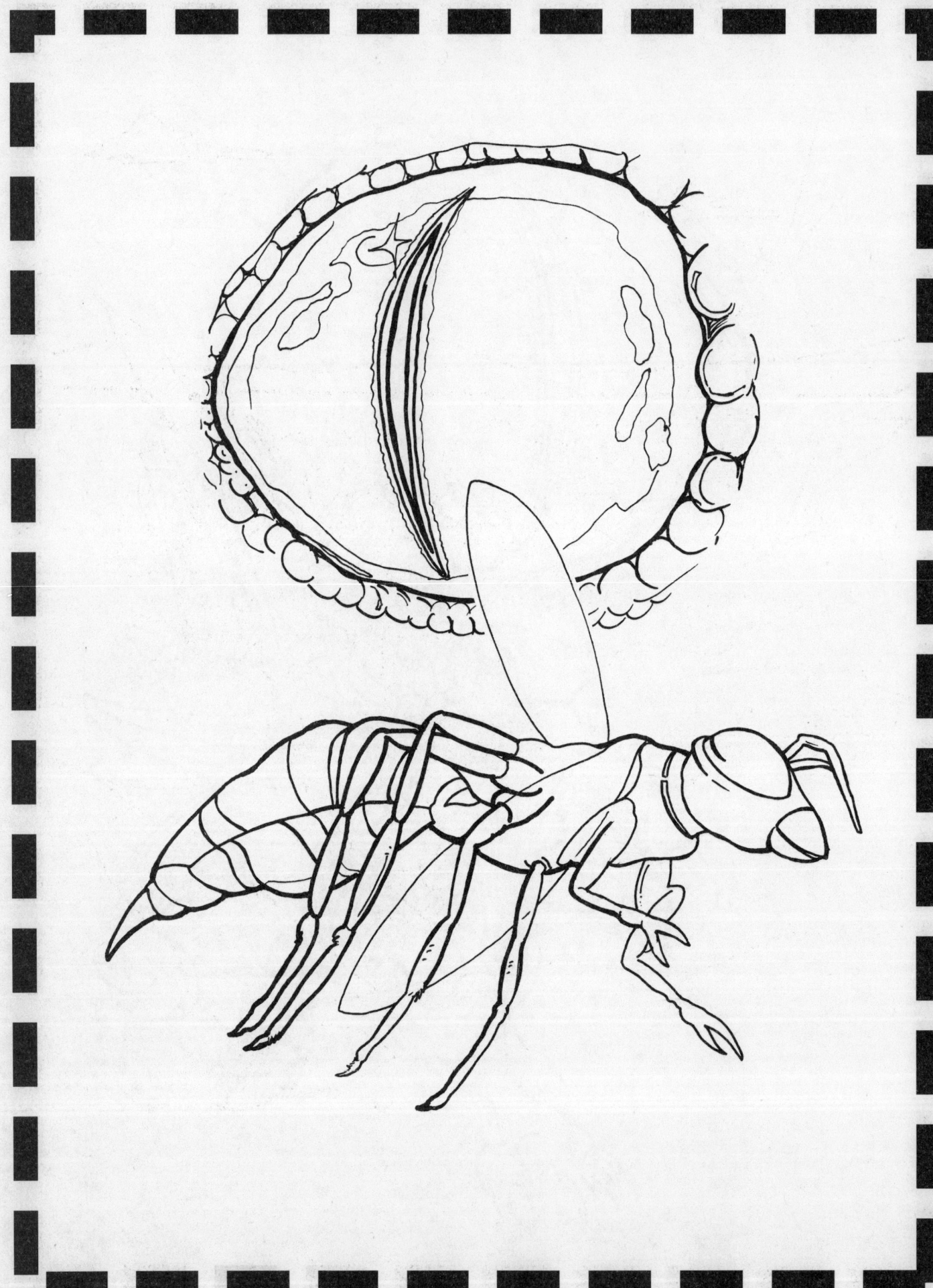

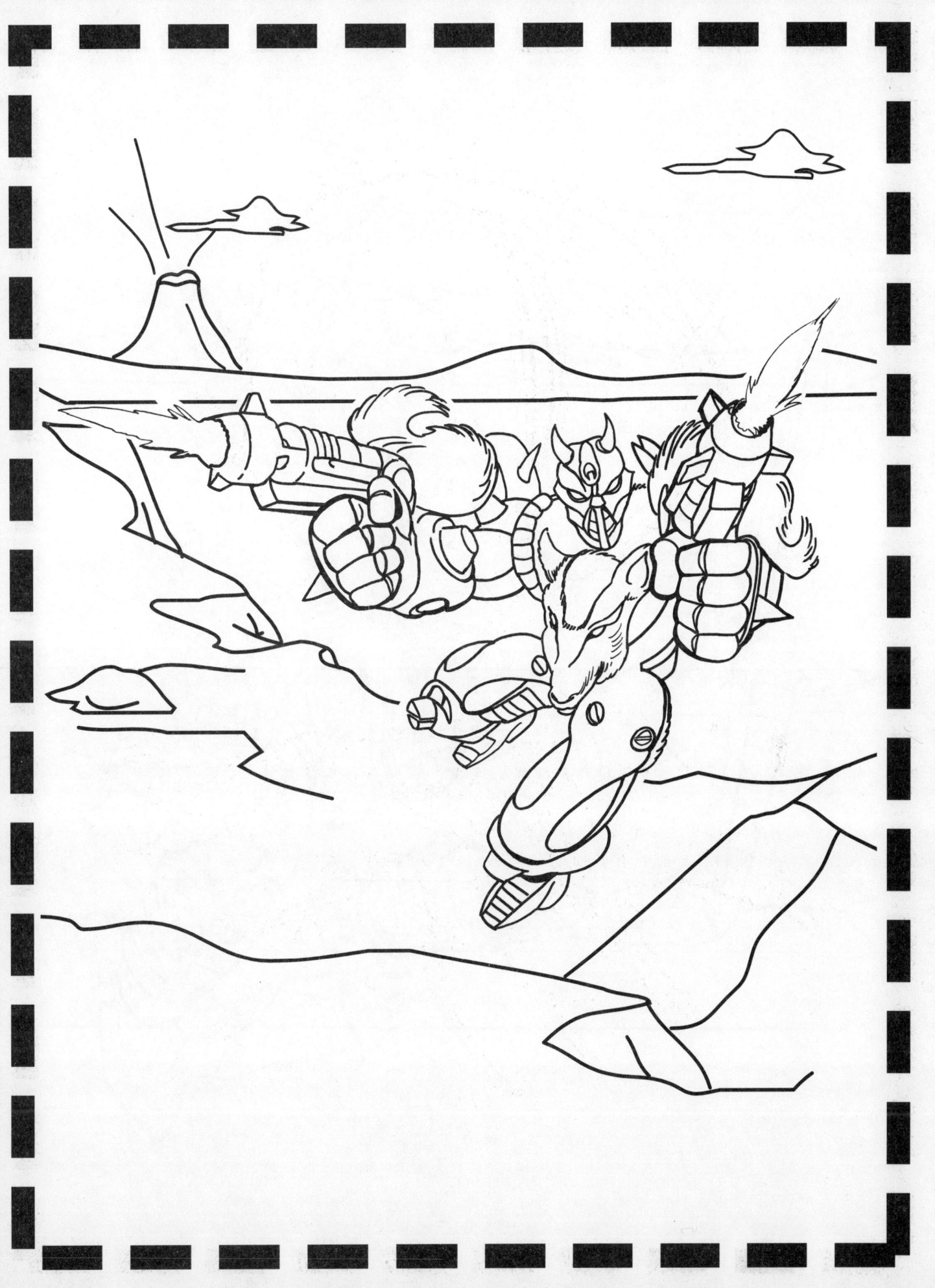

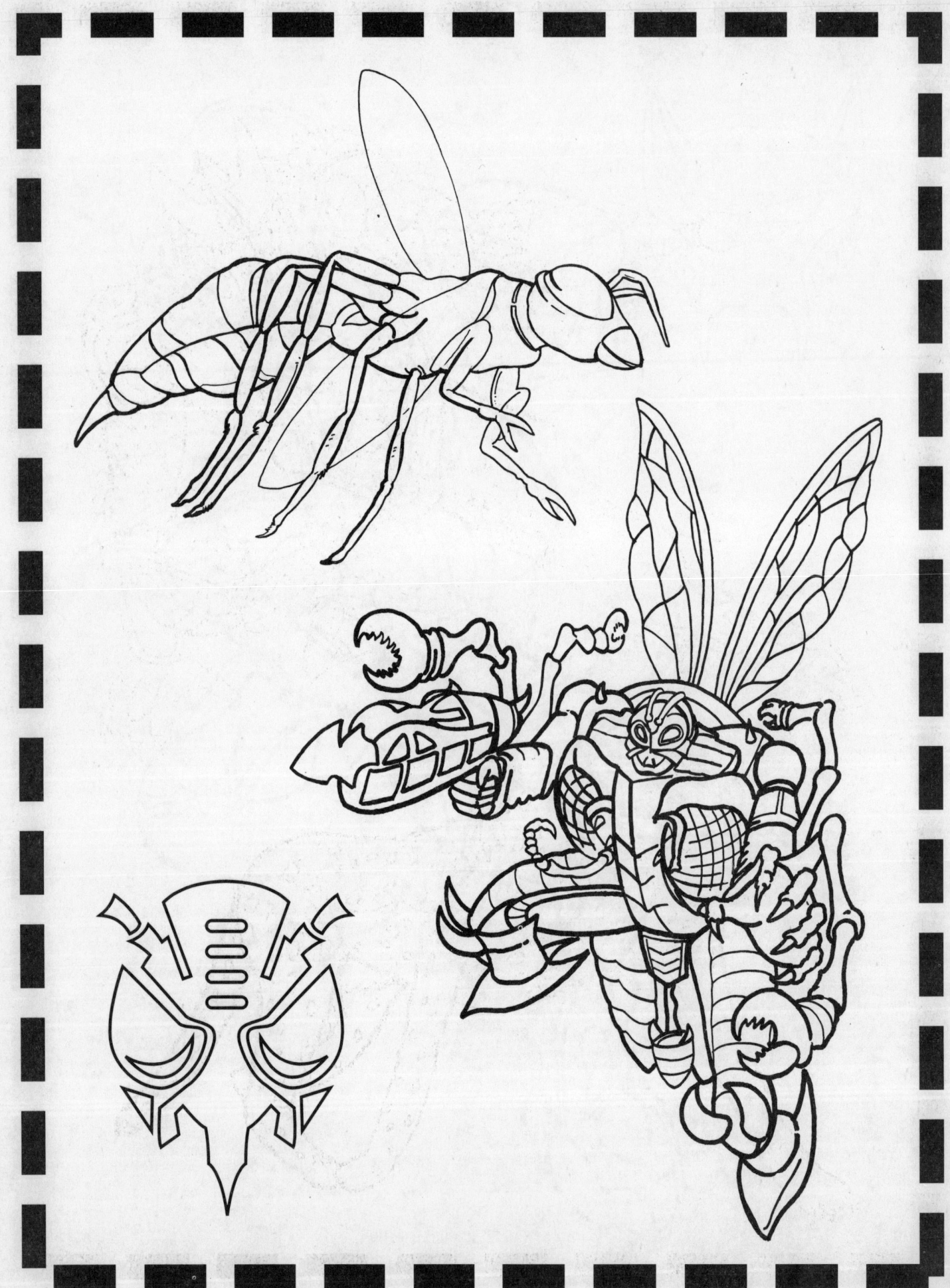

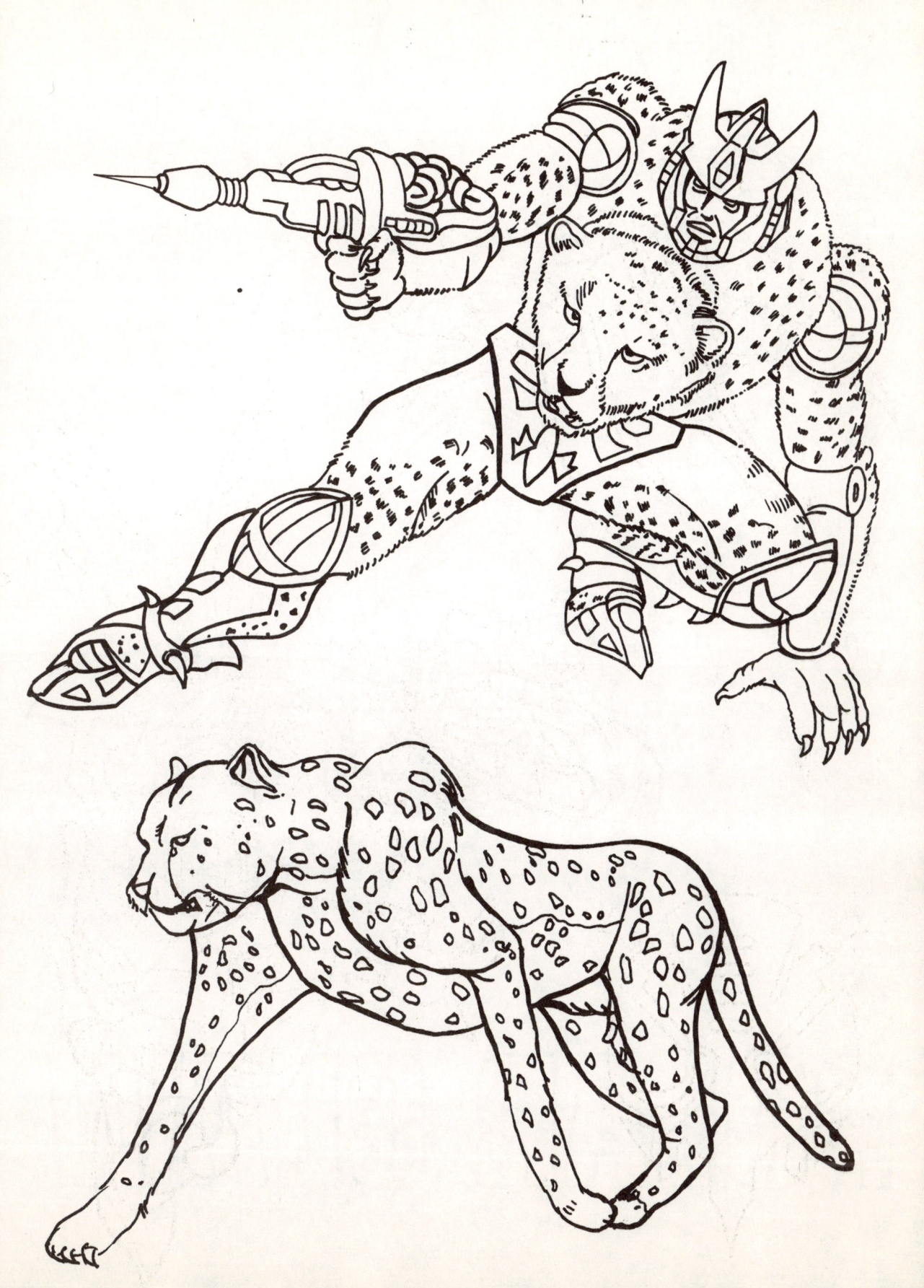

POLAR CLAW

IGUANA

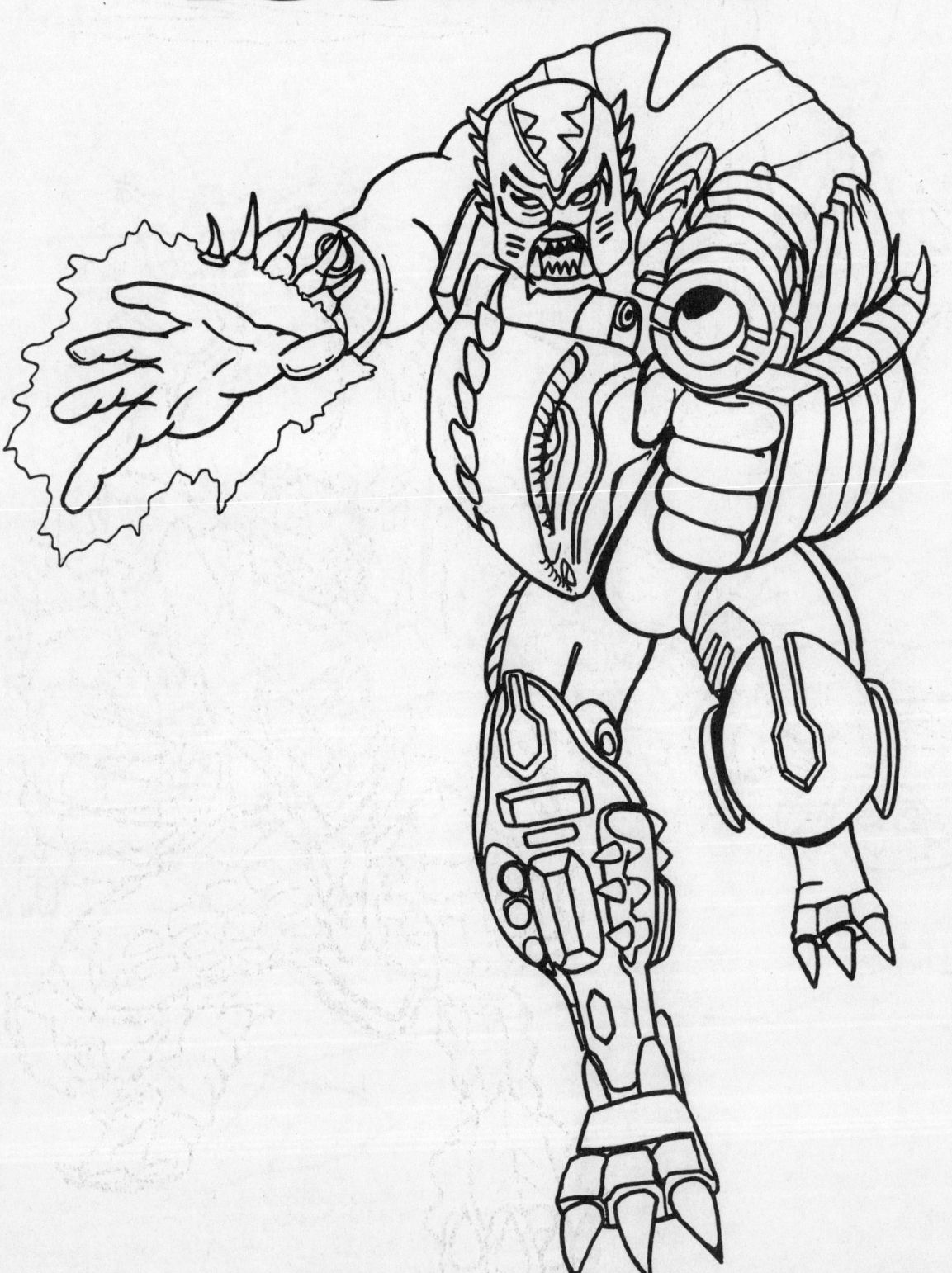

ARMORDILLO

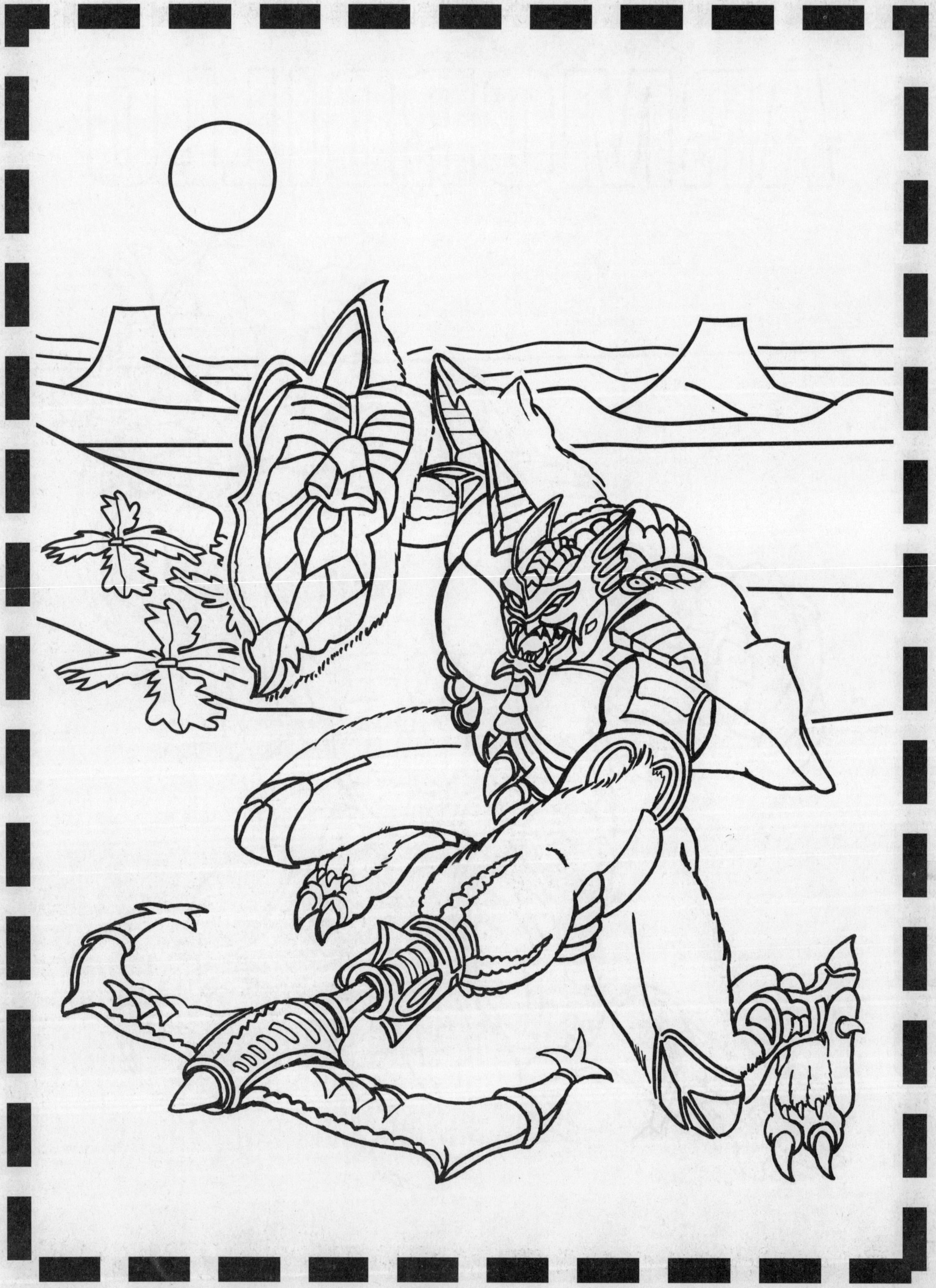

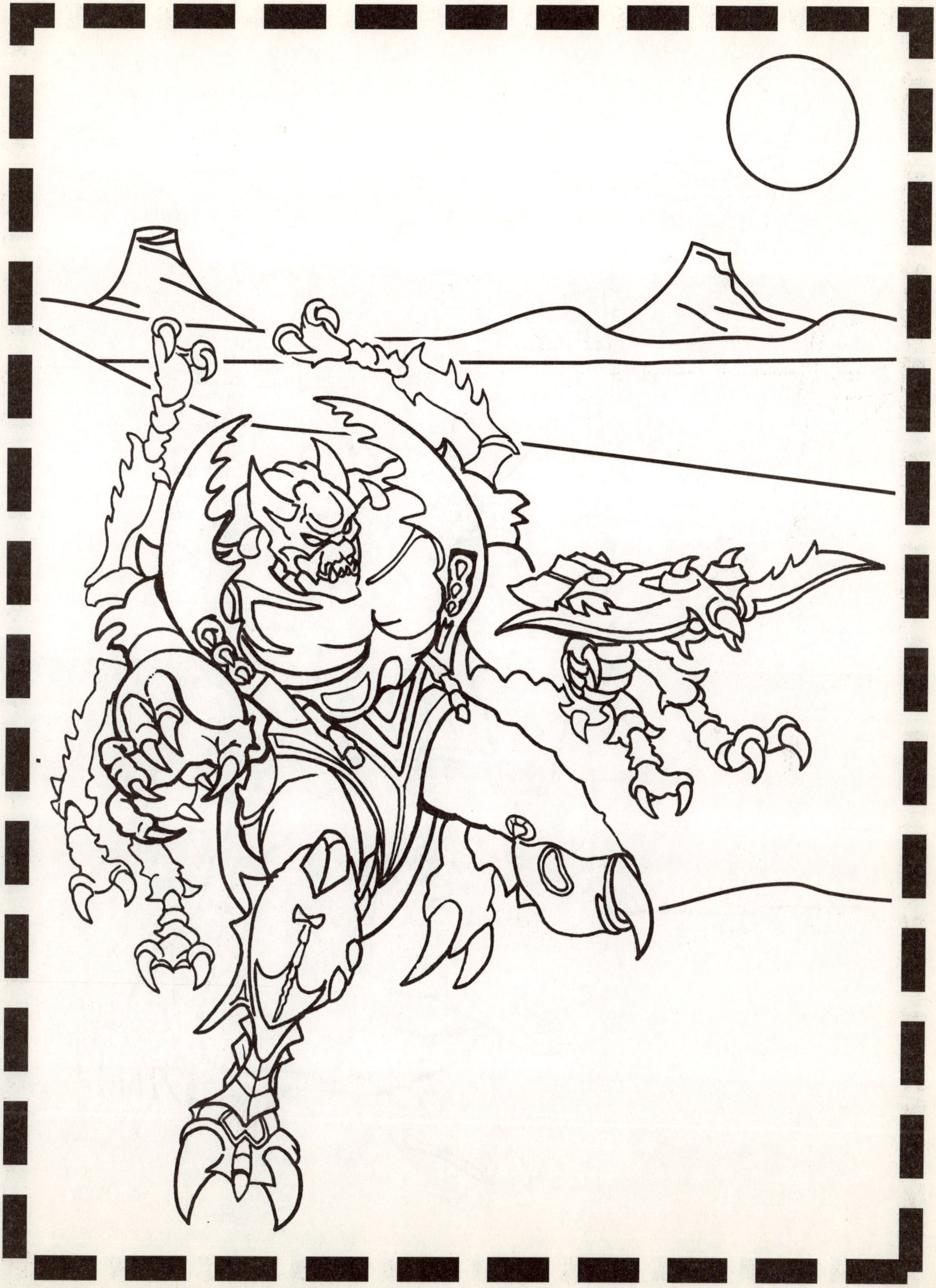

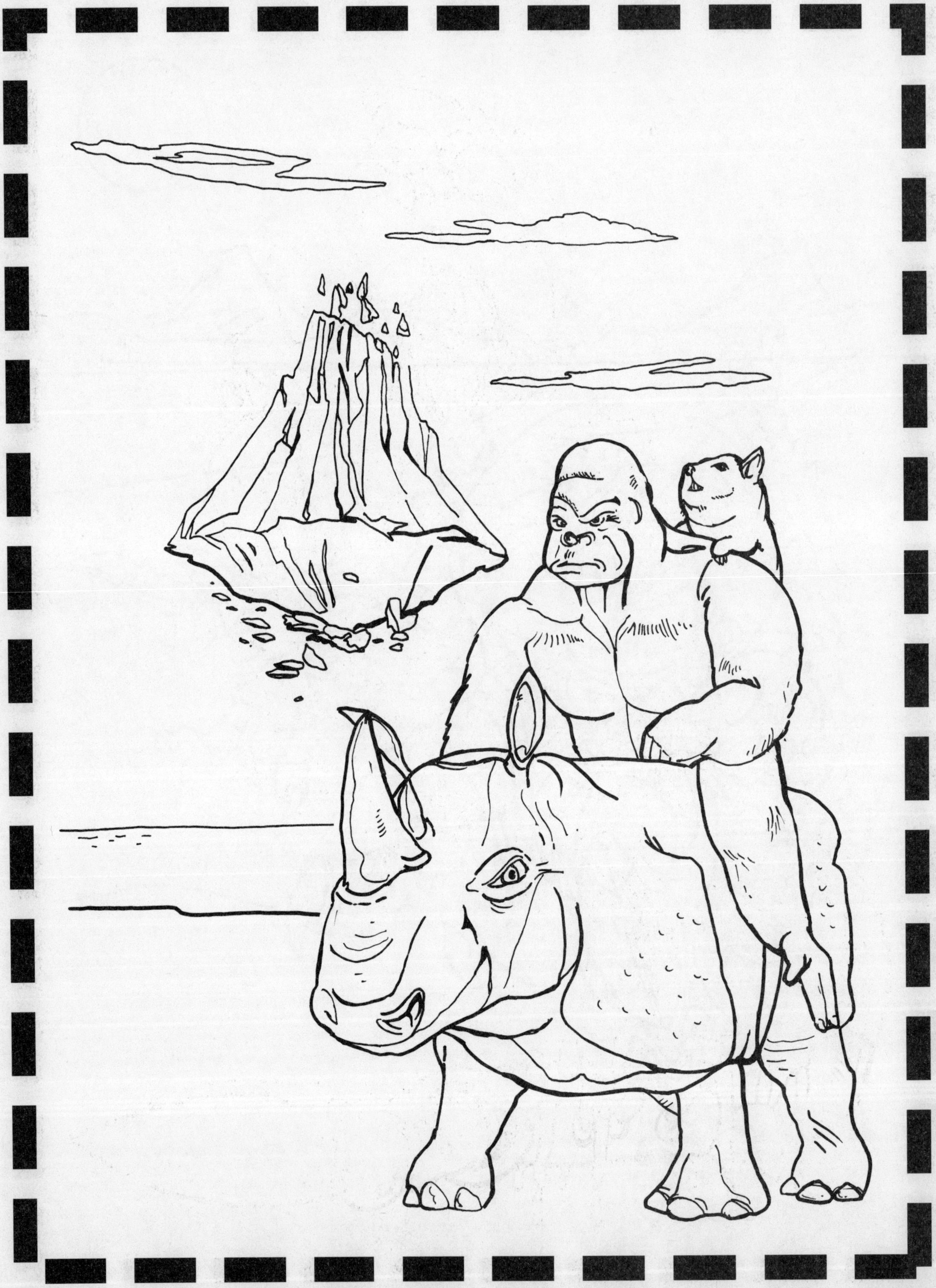

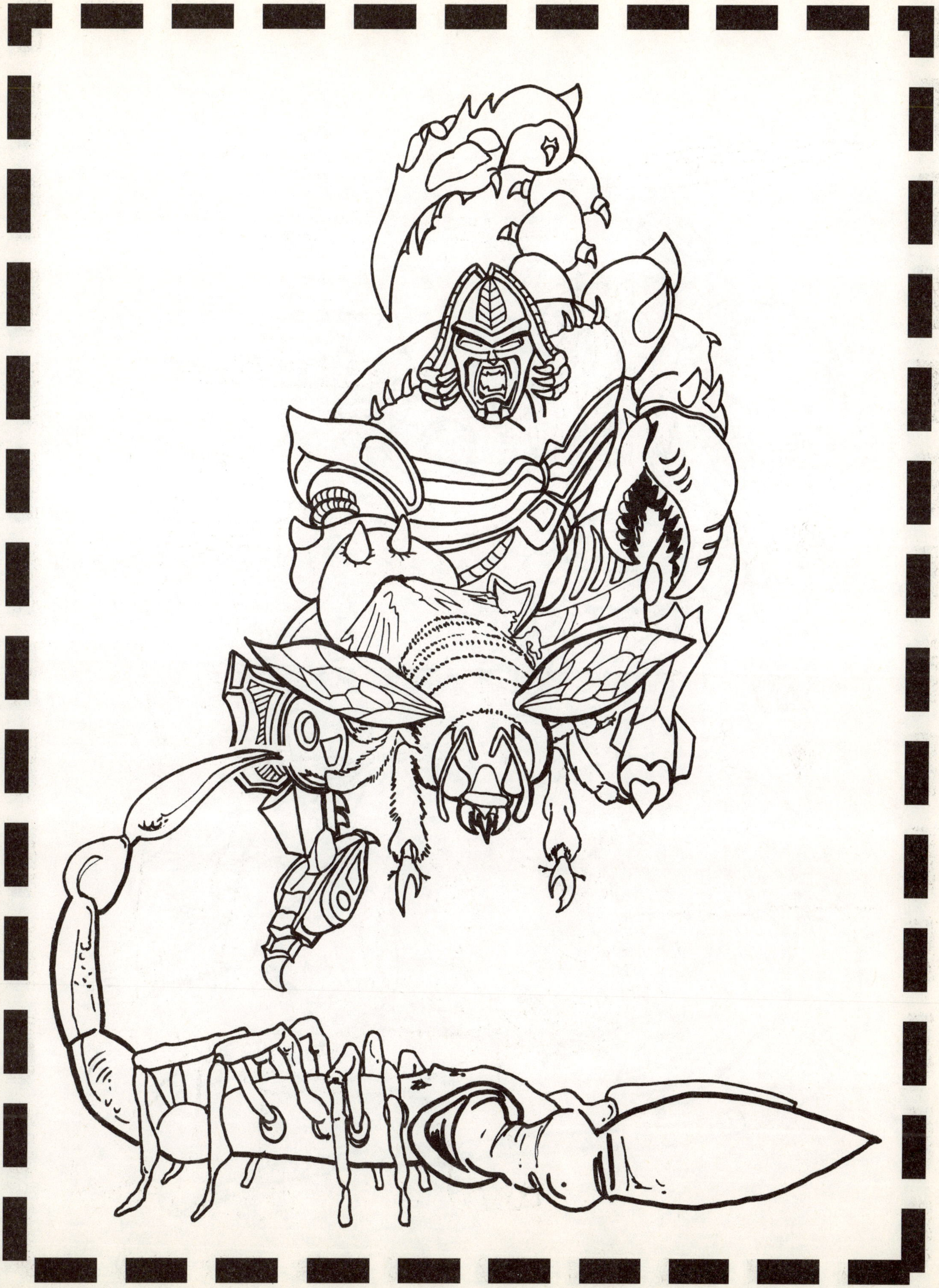

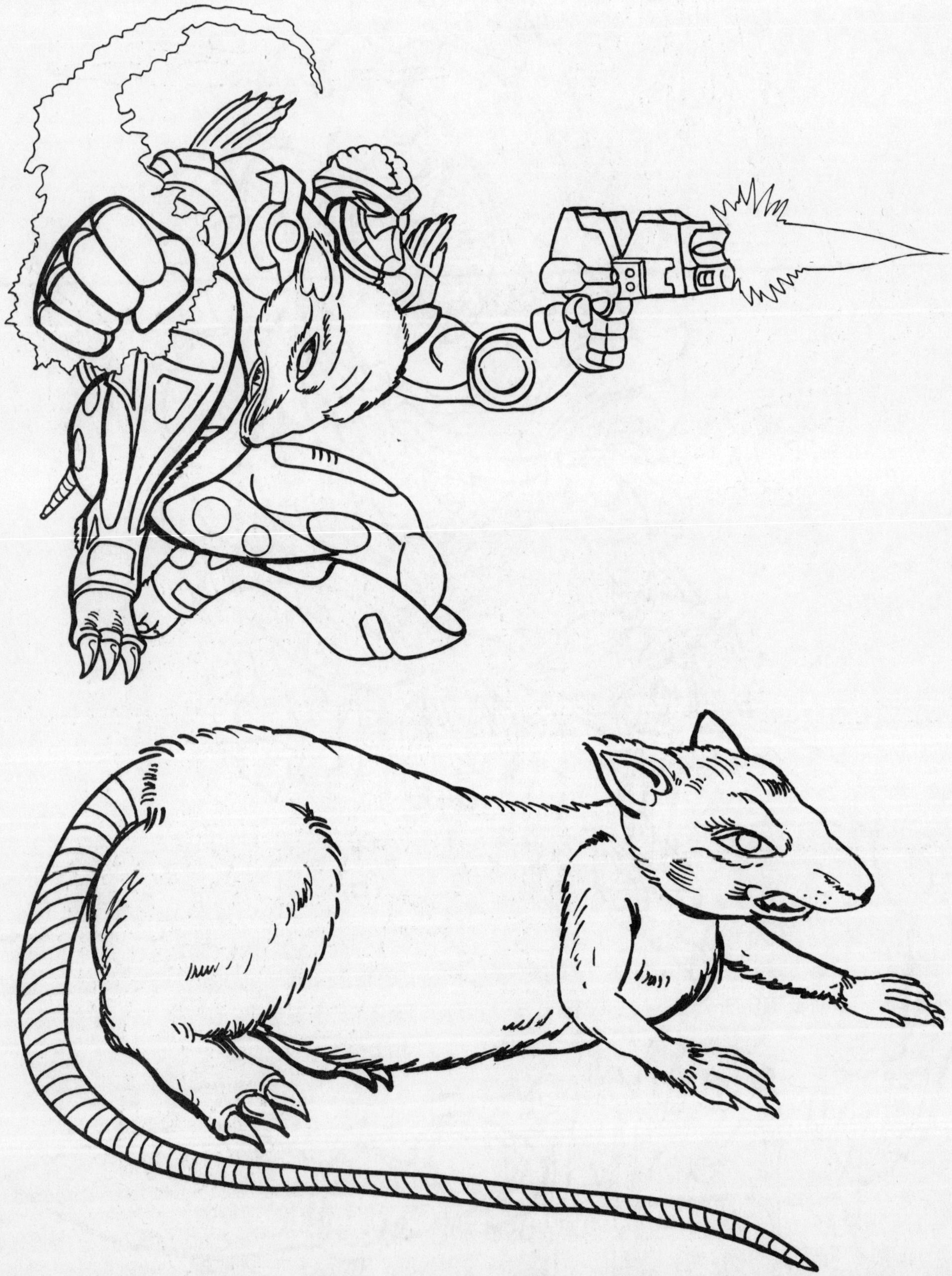

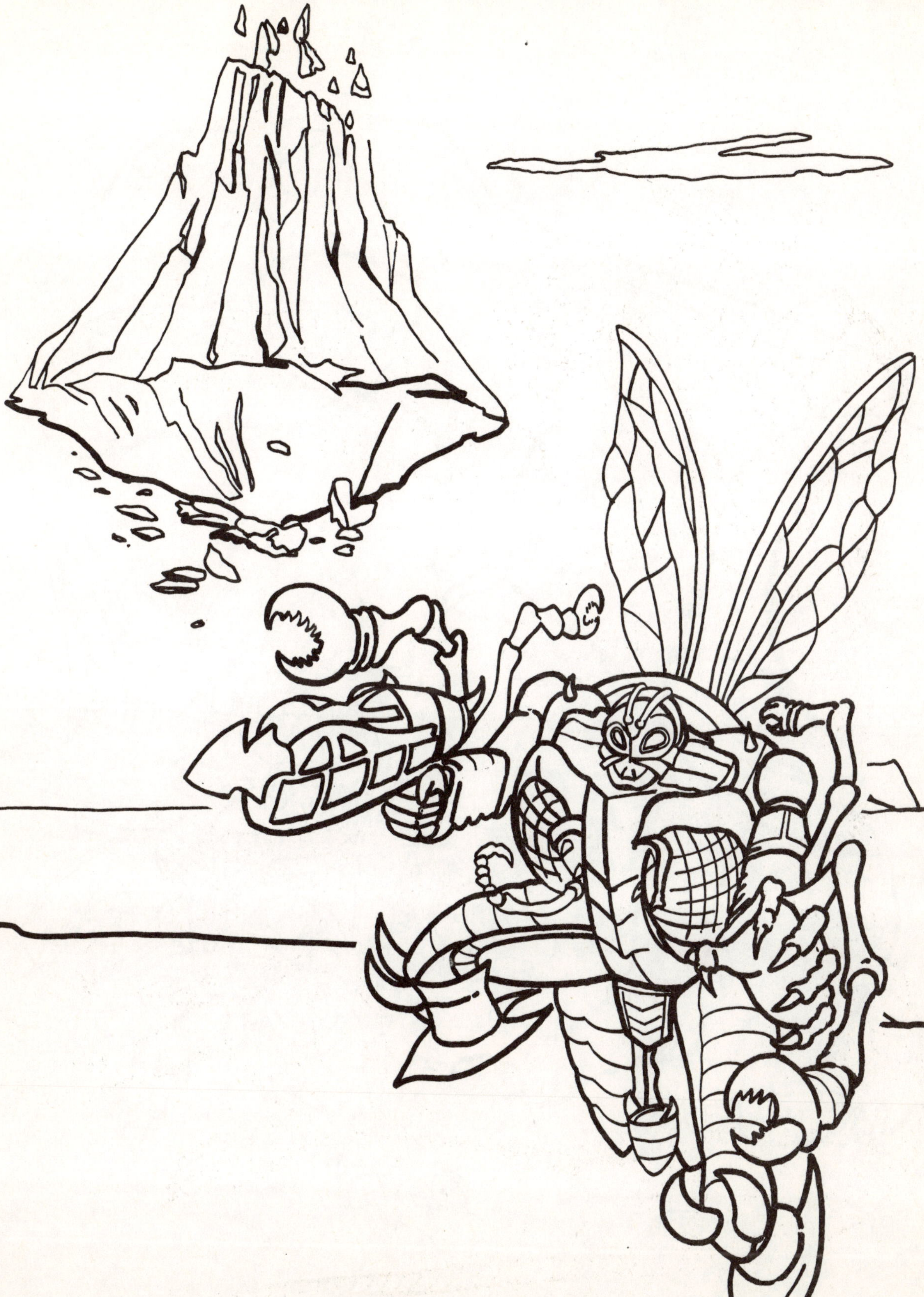

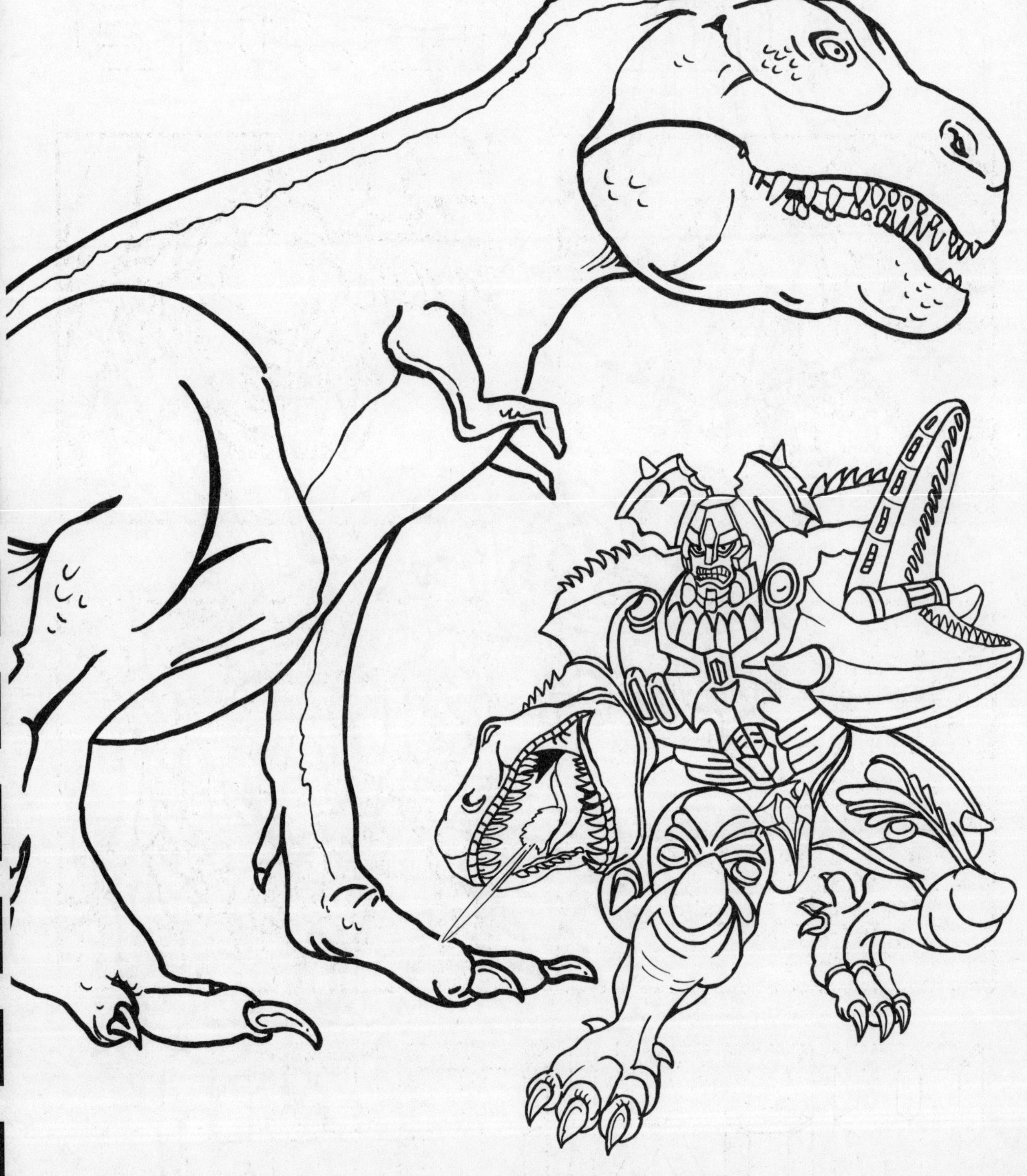

PREDACONS

MAXIMALS

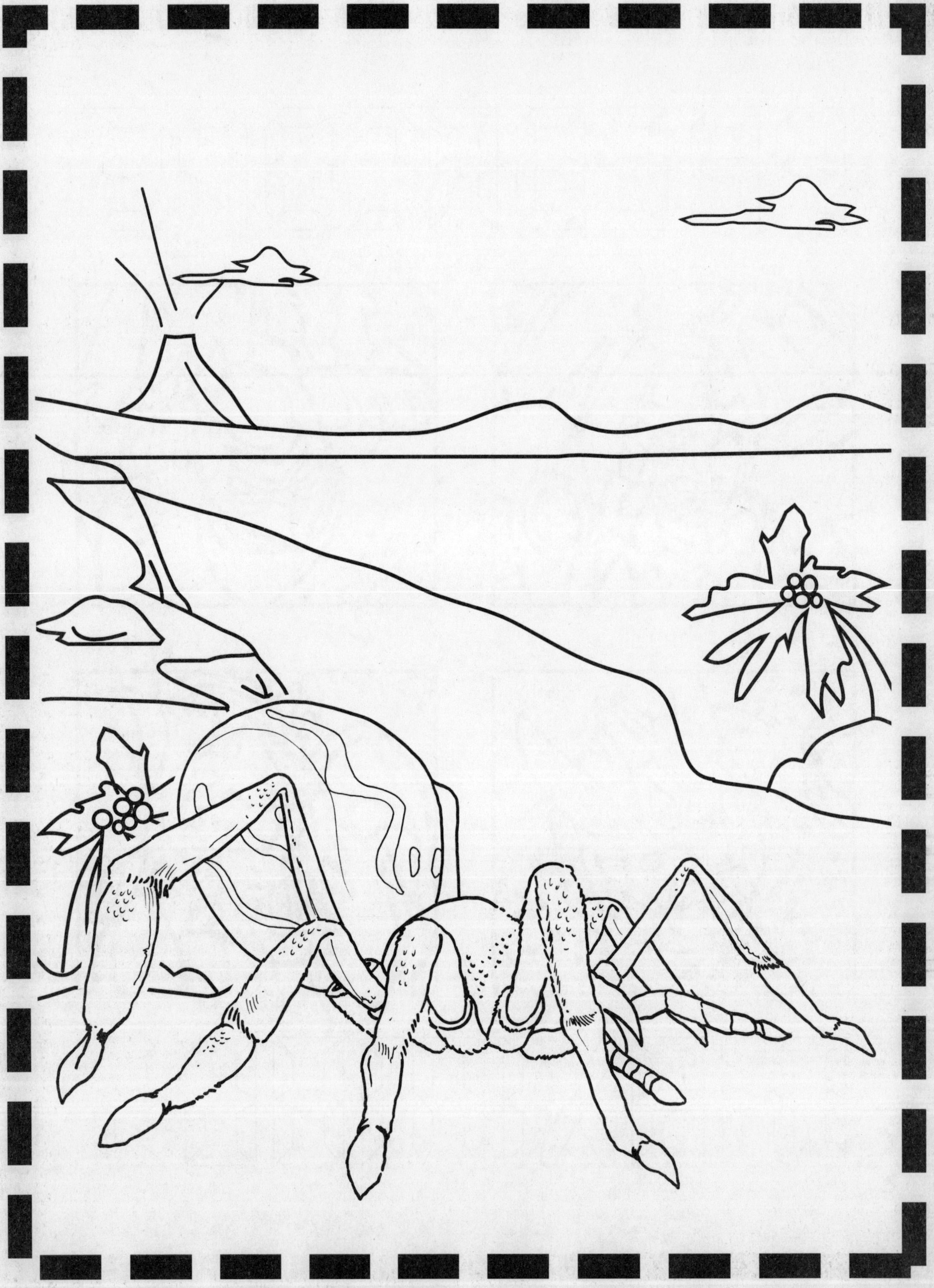